DIRECTOR'S CHOICE
KUTNÁ HORA – SEDLEC: CATHEDRAL AND OSSUARY

KUTNÁ HORA – SEDLEC: CATHEDRAL AND OSSUARY

Radka Krejčí

SCALA

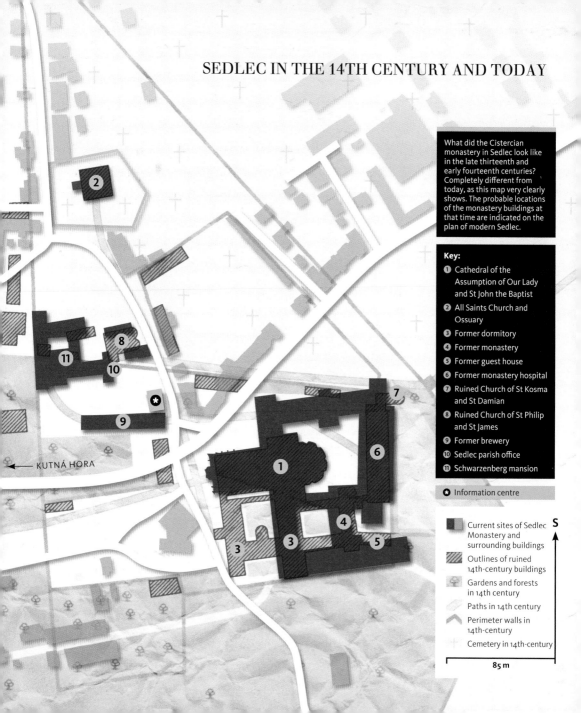

SEDLEC IN THE 14TH CENTURY AND TODAY

What did the Cistercian monastery in Sedlec look like in the late thirteenth and early fourteenth centuries? Completely different from today, as this map very clearly shows. The probable locations of the monastery buildings at that time are indicated on the plan of modern Sedlec.

Key:

1. Cathedral of the Assumption of Our Lady and St John the Baptist
2. All Saints Church and Ossuary
3. Former dormitory
4. Former monastery
5. Former guest house
6. Former monastery hospital
7. Ruined Church of St Kosma and St Damian
8. Ruined Church of St Philip and St James
9. Former brewery
10. Sedlec parish office
11. Schwarzenberg mansion

✪ Information centre

■ Current sites of Sedlec Monastery and surrounding buildings

▨ Outlines of ruined 14th-century buildings

Gardens and forests in 14th century

Paths in 14th century

Perimeter walls in 14th-century

Cemetery in 14th-century

← KUTNÁ HORA

S

85 m

CONTENTS

INTRODUCTION

When most foreign tourists hear the name Kutná Hora, they think of the famous ossuary in Sedlec, whereas most Czech visitors think of St Barbara's Church. The Cathedral of the Assumption of Our Lady and St John the Baptist in Sedlec remains, unjustly, somewhat in the shadow of these two Kutná Hora landmarks. But it was Sedlec Cathedral that formed the heart of the oldest Cistercian monastery within what is now the Czech Republic. Essentially, without Sedlec Monastery Kutná Hora itself would never have been built. In the second half of the thirteenth century, the Cistercian monks discovered silver deposits that sparked off a silver rush and the sudden expansion of the town of Kutná Hora.

Today, the imposing Cathedral of the Assumption of Our Lady and St John the Baptist is what mainly reminds us that the monastery here was once one of the most important in the Czech lands, welcoming the kings John of Luxembourg, Charles IV and Wenceslas IV as honoured guests. The site of the former dormitory is hidden behind a high wall, and the monastery's formerly compact magnificence has been definitively lost under layers of modern buildings, its location bisected by a main road that leads directly past the cathedral. Some of the monastery buildings, and their extensive parks and gardens, are also irrevocably lost, as is the Church of St Philip and St James, which used to stand halfway between the cathedral and the ossuary.

Nevertheless, Sedlec is one of the Czech Republic's most popular visitor attractions today. Visitors from all over the world are interested in coming here because of a tiny church standing in the middle of a small cemetery: All Saints Church and Ossuary. There are five hundred ossuaries in the Czech Republic, and this ossuary has yet to be granted national cultural monument status, yet the place attracts hundreds of thousands of visitors every year. Why? Because it is unique: no other ossuary uses human remains as a design element – or rather, as materials – to express the transience of human life and the hopeful nature of human existence in so artistic a fashion and with such great piety.

The western facade of the Cathedral of the Assumption of Our Lady and St John the Baptist

This profound truth is reflected in the ossuary's decorations, which are made from human bones. Some contemporary visitors may feel that treating human remains in this way is morbid, and indeed strange; other visitors, by contrast, are drawn by the bones and seek different explanations and hidden meanings in the symbols. Any explanation of why the ossuary was created, and of its mission, must be sought in the context of the period in which All Saints Church and Ossuary were constructed and decorated, and also in relation to the concept underlying the unique bone decorations.

All Saints Church was built as a practical solution to a problem encountered by many at the time, the Sedlec Cistercians included. The plague epidemics of the Middle Ages created huge pressure to bury many

people in an extremely short space of time, while still maintaining the necessary respect for human remains – even those disinterred from graves intended for repeated burials. Over time, a huge collection of human bones was amassed. The church has two floors for precisely this reason – the lower chapel lies below ground level and served as a reverential repository for bones, while the upper chapel is above ground and was used for praying for the dead. In the two towers above the upper chapel, a light burned incessantly as a symbol of hope in resurrection, and also as a navigational aid for the medieval pilgrims who headed to Sedlec Ossuary from all over Europe. Nowadays, it is no longer clear who started to create artistic compositions with the bones, nor do we know the exact number of bones stored.

Generally, however, the baroque architectural genius Jan Blažej Santini Aichel (1677–1723) is considered the first person to conceive the

The presbytery with altar in the upper chapel of All Saints Church and Ossuary; a restored baroque portable (known as a positive) organ stands on the left

idea of decorating Sedlec Ossuary – he wanted to highlight faith in God, in the spirit of the then-fashionable Baroque, and at the same time to create a theatrum mundi in the purist possible form. He began to use human bones, which at that time were probably not stored here as whole skeletons. In the nineteenth century, František Rint (1835–?), an artist of the Romantic period, entered into the spirit of Santini Aichel's baroque ideas. The current bone decorations in the lower chapel are a sort of baroque-style blend of fully Christian symbols and Romanticism, which, by contrast, accentuates human suffering and death. What is more, although Sedlec Ossuary harbours much more than piles of bones, modern visitors find the bone decorations very difficult to interpret. The ossuary's mission is frequently not understood, and the legacy of our forebears who lived and worked in Sedlec is sometimes disparaged.

Throughout the Middle Ages, Sedlec Ossuary was a popular place of pilgrimage, and it essentially remains so today. Only the times have changed, and the modern pilgrims with them. In the Middle Ages, death was a natural part of life, but today it is a taboo subject. We have, in a way, been torn away from death; we do not want to think about it. And while a relationship with God was a crucial facet of existence for medieval people, modern visitors often have little to no knowledge of the tenets of the Christian faith. In the Middle Ages, pilgrims travelled to the ossuary to pray silently; they were aware of their mortality, and they hoped for resurrection. Modern tourists come for entirely different reasons. The managers of this unique historical site aim to protect Sedlec Ossuary, explain to visitors the true legacy of this place of prayer, and find a balance between the ossuary as a popular tourist destination, a mass grave for our ancestors, and as an active Roman Catholic church – a place for meeting God.

When medieval pilgrims visited Sedlec, they certainly also visited the ossuary and found lodging and refreshment in the monastery buildings, but they could not enter the much-admired Cathedral of the Assumption of Our Lady because it was for Cistercian monks only. Today, the cathedral doors stand wide open as it is a parish church, a significant tourist destination, and a gallery of medieval and modern art.

So, let us walk together round both the mysterious Sedlec Ossuary and the Cathedral of the Assumption of Our Lady and St John the Baptist, the heart of Sedlec, which has held UNESCO World Heritage status since 1995.

1 THE FOUNDATION OF SEDLEC MONASTERY (1142–1282)

THE LEGEND DESCRIBING THE foundation of the first Cistercian monastery within what is now the Czech Republic runs as follows: 'During a long and tiring journey, Prince Miroslav was searching for a place to rest. He chose a forest clearing at the precise spot where Sedlec is located today. Here he lay down, put his head on his saddle, and fell asleep. His retinue then saw something very strange: a little white bird with golden wings flew into the prince's half-open mouth. After a moment, it flew out again, and Miroslav woke up, fully refreshed. He told his companions that he had had a vision in his dreams – an angel had visited him and proclaimed that he should consecrate a new monastery in this sacred place. Miroslav soon founded the monastery here in accordance with God's will. The place was called Sedlec, after the saddle [*sedlo* in Czech] he had rested his head on.'[1]

It was the great nobleman Miroslav who acquired the modern Sedlec region in the twelfth century and decided to found a Cistercian monastery

An archaeological survey revealing the foundations of a 12th-century Romanesque basilica in the cathedral's north aisle

The Foundation of the Cistercian Order and its Expansion around the World, by an unknown artist, in the side aisle (early 18th century)

here. The deeds of foundation were drawn up around 1145 (a facsimile is on display in Sedlec Cathedral treasury). The first twelve monks arrived in Sedlec about the same time. In addition to the Romanesque Church of the Assumption, which was built on the site of the modern cathedral, the Cistercians probably also built the adjacent dormitory and agricultural buildings. After 1278, however, the community's financial situation deteriorated with dire consequences: in 1281, the community was in danger of being dissolved completely.

Things took a turn for the better in 1282, when Heinrich Heidenreich was elected the monastery's new abbot and one of Sedlec's most glorious eras commenced.

Facsimile of the deeds of foundation of Sedlec Monastery. The original, drawn up around 1145, is held by the National Museum in Prague, inventory number 1

2 THE HEYDAY OF SEDLEC MONASTERY (1282–1320)

ONE OF THE LARGEST SEAMS of silver ore in Europe was discovered on the monastery's land in the time of Abbot Heidenreich, resulting in the foundation of the celebrated mining town of Kutná Hora. Although the silver found on the monastery's estates belonged to the monarch, the Cistercians had a right to a share of the revenues, amounting to a significant income. Abbot Heidenreich was able to take advantage of these funds, and Sedlec Monastery thus became the richest in the country.

Abbot Heidenreich was not only a talented economist, he was also a diplomat and a close friend of King Wenceslas II. The legend says that Heidenreich was sent by the king on a diplomatic journey to Jerusalem: 'On his journey to Jerusalem, he visited Calvary. There he took a handful of earth from the holy mountain and transported it home, where he scattered it over Sedlec Cemetery. From then on, many Christians from the region, and from faraway lands, sought the opportunity to be buried in this holy ground after their deaths. Burial in Sedlec meant being closer to the resurrection. Not without reason was the Sedlec Cemetery nicknamed the "Holy Field".'[2]

Heidenreich led Sedlec Monastery for forty years – a golden age. The entire monastery complex was rebuilt in the late thirteenth and early fourteenth centuries. Just thirty years later, the gothic Monastery Church of the Assumption of Our Lady was also built – at that time, the largest sacred building in the Czech lands. In about 1320, when Heidenreich died, the monastery's property included as many as fifty villages and at least ten farms. However, Heidenreich's death was followed by an economic crisis, which foreshadowed the monastery's decline.

3 THE DECLINE OF SEDLEC MONASTERY (1320–1421)

FINANCIAL DIFFICULTIES WERE looming even before Heidenreich died, but after his death these took on alarming proportions. High taxes were introduced during the rule of the king of Bohemia, John of Luxembourg (reigned 1310–46), and not even Sedlec Monastery could avoid them. At one point, the monastery was even unable to support its monks, who were forced to temporarily disperse to other monasteries. However, the monastery retained its prestigious position and was frequently visited by the country's important personalities.

Furthermore, Sedlec Monastery had a tense relationship with Kutná Hora. This culminated in 1412 with a conflict between the miners and the monastery's vassals. It ended when Malín, a nearby small town, was burned and its citizens were murdered.

However, the deepest crisis began on 24 April 1421, when the Hussites

Skulls displayed in a glass case in the lower chapel of All Saints Church and Ossuary, with evidence of injuries sustained in 1421, during a massacre of monks that took place during the Hussite Wars (1419–34)

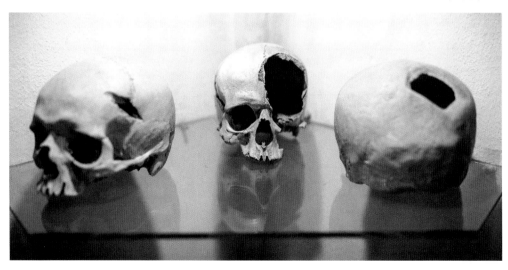

The Fire at Sedlec Monastery, by the baroque painter Michael Willmann, in the main nave (early 18th century)

DOUBLE-PAGE SPREAD, OVERLEAF: The remains of monks murdered in 1421 during the Hussite Wars are now reverently stored in one of the niches in the cathedral's side aisles. They seem to have been discovered during the reconstruction of the cathedral at the start of the 18th century

arrived, burned the complex and murdered the monks. Another legend is associated with this tragic event: 'Jan Žižka expressly forbade his troops to burn the Church of the Assumption of Our Lady. Nevertheless, one zealous warrior climbed onto the church roof and set it on fire. Sheriff Žižka is said to have taken the loss of the beautiful cathedral very hard indeed. He had it made known that he would richly reward the man who burned down the church with enough silver for the rest of his life, if he would only come forward. The perpetrator did so, and was seized and bound on the spot. Žižka had some silver melted and poured down the arsonist's throat.'[5]

After the monastery was destroyed by fire, Sedlec would not be revived until the first half of the sixteenth century.

4 ABBOT JINDŘICH SNOPEK AND THE REVIVAL OF SEDLEC MONASTERY (1685–1709)

JINDŘICH SNOPEK WAS BORN into a poor farming family in 1651. At the age of 20, he joined the Cistercian monastery at Sedlec, and when he was 35 he was elected its abbot. He was the main driving force behind the reconstruction of both the monastery and the cathedral, which had been left in ruins after the Hussite raids.

Yet another interesting legend relates how Snopek managed to obtain sufficient funds for reviving Sedlec: 'One day in 1703, a strange thing happened. As Abbot Jindřich went to oversee the building workers, an old, shabby beggar approached and greeted him. The abbot was already reaching for some alms, but the beggar himself gave him a kreuzer [a relatively low-value coin] and earnestly begged that he would accept it as an honest gift towards the church building costs. The abbot did not scorn this modest gift, instead he used it to buy a glass circle that he had inserted into one of the windows. The legend goes on to say that, from the day on which the abbot accepted the beggar's money, donations to the church grew rapidly. As early as 1707, the church had not only been successfully constructed, but also richly decorated with furnishings and valuable paintings.'[4]

The truth is that the cathedral restoration began in 1699 (some sources state as early as 1694) and was completed in 1709. However, Abbot Snopek did not live to see the cathedral completed and consecrated. Unfortunately, the costly repairs to the cathedral and dormitory brought the monastery to financial ruin; it was definitively dissolved less than eighteen years after the cathedral had been ceremonially reconsecrated.

A memorial stone to Jindřich Snopek (1651–1709) can be found on the right-hand side of the Chapel of the Fourteen Holy Helpers, bearing the inscription *Restaurator Magnificus*, or Great Restorer

LEFT: The reliquary of St Vincent, a Roman martyr, a gift to the cathedral from Pope Benedict XIV on the occasion of the 600th anniversary of his sanctification

BELOW LEFT: The reliquary of St Felix and, above it, *The Last Eucharist of St Benedict*, by Jan Kryštof Liška (early 18th century)

BELOW RIGHT: The reliquary of St Vincent and, above it, *St Bernard Nursed by Wisdom*, by Jan Kryštof Liška (early 18th century)

The cathedral's loft, which is open to the public and can be accessed as far as the choir, contains a pillar carved with a small figure, probably by one of the labourers who worked on the cathedral's Baroque restoration (1699–1709)

RIGHT: Sedlec Cathedral is built on the ground plan of a Roman cross. At the crossing (where the nave and transept meet), there are frescos by Johann Jakob Stevens von Steinfels (1706) depicting the three persons of the Trinity: God the Father, God the Son – Jesus Christ – and God the Holy Spirit

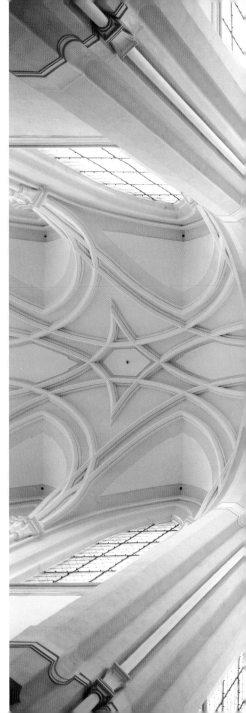

The Chapel of the Fourteen Holy Helpers in the north aisle. The first attempts to restore the cathedral after the Hussite Wars began here in 1699

5 THE DISSOLUTION OF SEDLEC MONASTERY (1764 – LATE 19th CENTURY)

View of the north transept (nave) with a wooden statue of Christ on the cross and behind it, a painting, The Assumption of the Virgin Mary, by Joseph Bergler the Younger (1803)

IN AUTUMN 1785, when Sedlec Monastery was more than six hundred years old, Joseph II, Holy Roman Emperor, issued a decree dissolving all contemplative convents and monasteries. The enforced dissolution, however, was no more than the proverbial *coup de grâce*. The monastery was drowning in debts arising from mismanagement of the monumental restoration project. Matters were not helped by the scandal surrounding the last abbot, Xaver Freisauf (1710–1780), who in 1764 ran away with his mistress and some stolen monastery property to Germany, where he converted to Protestantism. A few years later, he asked for forgiveness and was permitted to return to the monastic community in Sedlec.

After the monastery was dissolved, the cathedral was deconsecrated and began to be used as a storehouse. The monastery's huge debts were partially discharged by an auction of its property in 1786, in which magnificent artistic artefacts were sold off, mostly for significantly less than their value. In 1801, the cathedral became the parish church for Sedlec and Malín. The former monastery lands were bought by Karl Philipp, prince of Schwarzenberg, who converted the old prelature building into a mansion. The Schwarzenberg family also assumed the patronage of All Saints Church and Ossuary and launched extensive repairs. In 1817, the Church of St Philip and St James was demolished. A tobacco manufacturer from the town of Golčův Jeníkov moved into the dormitory building in 1812 – the company is still based there today, albeit under different ownership. The monastery complex gradually lost its integrity, which allowed the Imperial road leading right through the site to be constructed in the early nineteenth century. The original grounds, which were firmly enclosed by fortification walls, would be lost under new developments throughout the nineteenth century.

6 THE FORMER SEDLEC MONASTERY SITE IN THE 20TH AND 21ST CENTURIES

THROUGHOUT MOST OF THE twentieth century, the former Sedlec Monastery site fell into disrepair, as a result of the political and social events within what is now the Czech Republic. The original Cistercian site did not suffer any serious damage during the First and Second World Wars; the greatest devastation to both sacred buildings (the cathedral and the ossuary) occurred mainly after 1948, when both the will and the means were lacking for even basic maintenance. The final blow was delivered in 1978, when a major road was built in the immediate vicinity of the cathedral.

From 1948 to 1989, the ossuary was open to visitors and the cathedral was used as the working church of Sedlec parish. By 1989, both of Sedlec's

View of the courtyard of the Schwarzenberg mansion built in the 19th century on the site of Sedlec Monastery's new prelature building

The administrative building in the grounds of the Schwarzenberg mansion

Remains of a baroque entrance gate to the Sedlec monastery lands and the original perimeter walls

sacred monuments had gone to rack and ruin. The Cathedral of the Assumption of Our Lady and St John the Baptist was, as the parish church, prioritised for renovations, particularly as it had gained UNESCO World Heritage status in 1995. The cathedral renovations began in 1999 and were completed in 2009. The restoration of the ossuary commenced in 2014 and is still ongoing.

In 1992, the Philip Morris Group became the owner of the tobacco factory based in the former monks' dormitory; the factory complex was expanded to the east and the Baroque dormitory building was repaired. It now houses the company's offices.

The Schwarzenberg family mansion, like the other farm buildings, was confiscated from the owners after 1948 and used by the agricultural cooperative from the nearby town of Čáslav. After 1989, the buildings were returned to the Schwarzenberg family in a very poor condition. A full architectural study for revitalising the entire property is currently being conducted.

Fragment of the original Romanesque monastery wall

BELOW AND OPPOSITE: the Schwarzenberg mansion, which was created in the 19th century on the site of Sedlec Monastery's prelature building

7 THE CATHEDRAL OF THE ASSUMPTION OF OUR LADY AND ST JOHN THE BAPTIST

THE FORMER MONASTERY CHURCH of the Assumption of Our Lady and St John the Baptist became a UNESCO World Heritage site in 1995. The original gothic basilica was erected in the late thirteenth and early fourteenth centuries during the monastery's heyday under Abbot Heidenreich. He had regularly visited France, becoming familiar with gothic architecture. When completed, the immense church was the largest sacred building in central Europe.

The cathedral was constructed on the site of the original Romanesque basilica, as testified by the discoveries made during an archaeological survey of the cathedral's north aisle. The original gothic church was built as a three-nave basilica with a transept and choir, a surrounding ambulatory and perimeter chapels. The architect of the gothic building was probably Petrus Delphini, and the building works were completed within an incredible thirty years, in line with his unified architectural plan.

In 1421, the whole monastery was destroyed by plundering Hussite troops; only the cathedral's outside walls were left standing. Reconstruction could not begin until the late seventeenth and early eighteenth centuries, when the then abbot, Jindřich Snopek, obtained sufficient funds. Snopek wanted to retain the cathedral's original gothic character, thus referencing Sedlec Monastery's glorious past. In 1702, he hired the young architect Jan Blažej Santini Aichel to take charge of the reconstruction.

The Cathedral of the Assumption of Our Lady and St John the Baptist, view from the north-west

The result of this daring choice was an exceptional work of architecture that made young Santini Aichel's name, and in which he pioneered some novel architectural ideas.

Despite the dissolution of the monastery and the turbulent history of the twentieth century, the cathedral remains true to Santini Aichel's vision today. Only the interior decoration has changed: it used to be painted a rich green, and the original furnishings are now largely missing because they were sold off at auction.

ABOVE LEFT: View from the presbytery into the main nave

ABOVE RIGHT: View from the choir loft into the main nave

The cathedral is 92 metres long in total.

The main altar in neo-gothic style; in the foreground, the original baroque tiles by Jan Blažej Santini Aichel

BELOW LEFT: A new organ, dating from 2009, is located in the cathedral's southern transept. It was inserted into the original, early 20th-century organ case, made by the Kutná Hora organ builder Josef Melzer

BELOW RIGHT: Sedlec Cathedral's ambulatory with radiating chapels viewed from the former dormitory. The cloister garden is in the foreground, and the former monastery buildings are to the sides

8   JAN BLAŽEJ SANTINI AICHEL (1677–1723)

WHEN ABBOT JINDŘICH SNOPEK hired the young Jan Blažej Santini Aichel, who was only 25, to restore the Cathedral of the Assumption of Our Lady, he would have had no idea of how famous and highly regarded this youth would become over the following years. It was in Sedlec that Santini Aichel unleashed his artistic genius, endless imagination and feeling for architecture.

Santini Aichel was born with a physical disability and was partially paralysed, so he was unable to follow in his father's footsteps as a stonemason. In addition to the stonemasonry of his forebears, he was also educated in painting by the French architect and painter Jean Baptiste Mathey (1630–1696); he studied descriptive geometry and was ambitious and determined. As a child, he explored the gothic architecture of St Vitus's Cathedral in Prague; while travelling in Italy, he familiarised himself with the Baroque architecture of Francesco Borromini (1599–1667), and later put all of this into practice in his own architectural projects.

During his relatively short professional career, Santini Aichel designed and built more than eighty buildings in Bohemia and Moravia. He planned his projects with a pair of compasses on flat paper, using the golden

OPPOSITE: A staircase in the dormitory designed by Jan Blažej Santini Aichel (early 18th century)

ABOVE: The laevorotatory staircase leading to the transept, one of the most important architectural elements by Jan Blažej Santini Aichel

ratio and whole numbers in the radii of individual circles. Santini Aichel's compasses thus created a construction diagram that resembled a kind of abstract network connecting interior and exterior, one that made maximum use of light as a symbol of the Divine. Santini Aichel was not only an architectural genius but also a devout Christian; records of the period describe him holding long conversations with the abbot and prelates of the monastery so he could perfect his work in all its forms in symbiosis with his faith.

The project to restore Sedlec Cathedral was what brought Santini Aichel fame, experience and testimonials, and the cathedral was also where he could, for the first time, put into practice the principles that he later developed in other constructions.

The dextrorotatory staircase leading to the transept (early 18th century) – one of the most important architectural elements introduced by Jan Blažej Santini Aichel

The baroque tiles in the presbytery, by the architectural genius Jan Blažej Santini Aichel

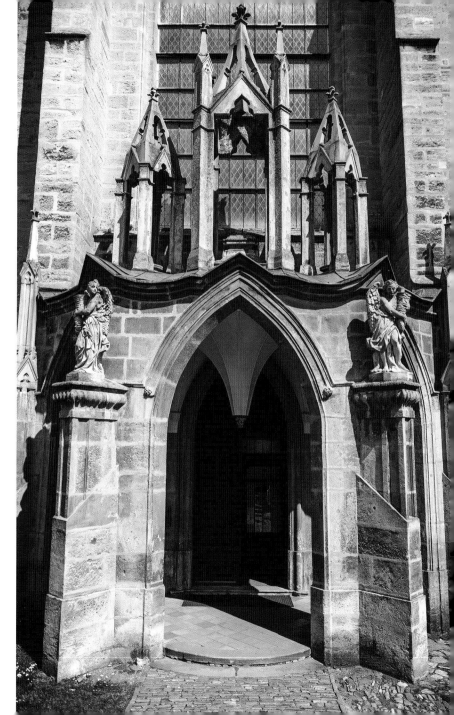

The architectural concept of the main entrance, designed by Jan Blažej Santini Aichel (early 18th century), was reputedly inspired by the shape of the Sedlec Monstrance

9 SANTINI AICHEL'S LEGACY IN SEDLEC

THE YOUNG SANTINI AICHEL arrived in Sedlec in 1702 as the project architect for the restoration of Sedlec Church, which by then had been in ruins for almost three hundred years. During the reconstruction, the main nave of the cathedral was vaulted with a Bohemian sail vault (a type of vault specific to baroque-gothic architecture) and decorated with a network of non-load-bearing ribbed stucco mouldings, connected to the gothic engaged columns. The architect intentionally did not include ribs in the central vaulted field at the crossing, in order to make space for the frescos. The side aisle was vaulted with Bohemian sail vaults. Further masterly architectural elements are the two elegantly self-supporting spiral staircases leading to the cathedral loft. Santini Aichel added a canopied vestibule to the

OPPOSITE: The hanging bone decoration representing a flying angel, suspended from the arched vault of the lower chapel of All Saints Church and Ossuary, with typical baroque stucco in the background, both by Jan Błażej Santini Aichel (early 18th century)

LEFT: View of the stucco ceiling decorations and choir loft in the vestibule of All Saints Church and Ossuary

ABOVE: Sedlec Cathedral has a cruciform ground plan. Frescos (1706) by Johann Jakob Stevens von Steinfels are located at the crossing

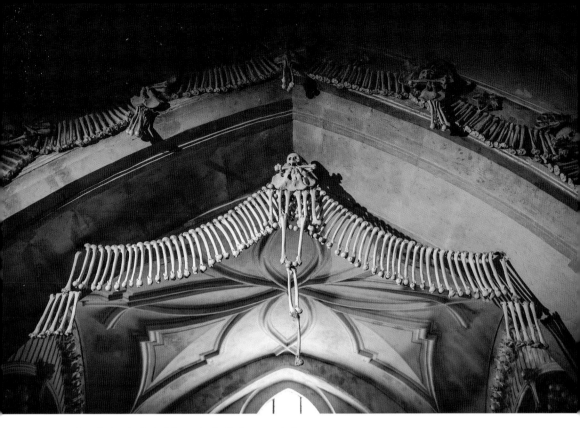

western façade that included the cathedral's largest window, in which he used the motif of a suspended apex stone for the first time. He put quatrefoils (a stylised representation of a flower with four petals) into the shields on the façade; gothic architecture routinely used quatrefoils in window tracery. Modern Kutná Hora has a quatrefoil as its logo.

When restoring the cathedral, Santini Aichel fully respected the instructions of Abbot Snopek: to retain the building's original gothic character – thus honouring the original builders and the tradition of the Cistercian order – but also to use modern baroque elements to proclaim the return of piety. By bringing these two seemingly incompatible styles together, he created a harmonious whole, and invented a distinctive new style: baroque-gothic.

The Bohemian sail vault (seen from the top), which Jan Błażej Santini Aichel used to cover the cathedral's side aisles

Abbot Snopek died in 1709. A year later, Santini Aichel was invited by the new abbot, Bonifatius Blahna, to restore All Saints Church and Ossuary. The gifted architect is also thought to have conceived the basic concept of the contemporary bone decorations in the spirit of piety and as an expression of the baroque aesthetic. As well as working with bones, he decorated the lower chapel with stucco and, because of excessive subsidence, he added a new foyer to the church, which was intended to stop the building from leaning to the west.

LEFT: View of the north aisle covered by the Bohemian sail vault

RIGHT: View of the vaulting over the nave and the stucco decoration by Jan Blażej Santini Aichel (early 18th century)

10   PETR BRANDL (1668–1735)

St Lawrence's Church in Vysoké Mýto. Petr Brandl's Baroque altarpiece, *The Assumption of the Virgin Mary* (1728), was originally painted for the main altar of the Cathedral of the Assumption of Our Lady in Sedlec

PETR BRANDL IS CONSIDERED one of the most important Czech baroque artists and also as one of the most infamous *enfants terribles* in the history of Czech painting. By the standards of the period, he pocketed incredible fees for his works, which he painted for the most important noble families and monasteries. However, he was also a terrible spendthrift and left debts wherever he went: for fine wine imported from the Canary Islands, clothing he commissioned from most expensive tailors, his Artists' Guild membership fees and also maintenance for his children. After several years of marriage to the Bohemian (in every sense of the term) painter, his exasperated wife Helena left her husband, even considering a legal separation in 1721.

Brandl was the youngest of six children born to a not-particularly affluent family. He failed to complete his studies at a Jesuit high school, but due to his extraordinary artistic talent was apprenticed to Christian Schröder, the court painter who worked at the Prague Castle Picture Gallery. Here he became familiar with the work of Dutch and Italian masters – this knowledge, because he himself never travelled abroad, was an important source of inspiration for him. Shortly after completing his apprenticeship, he started to win interesting commissions and also an increasing reputation as an excellent painter and incorrigible *enfant terrible*.

The painter's wild lifestyle was certainly reflected in the varying quality of his work. Nevertheless, his original brushwork, his habit of carving his paintings with the wooden brush-handle to achieve the desired spatial effect, his use of light and chiaroscuro, along with his novel composition, all make Brandl an important baroque artist in both the Czech and the central European contexts.

11   BRANDL'S WORK IN SEDLEC

The Patrons of the Czech Lands (c.1728) by
Petr Brandl, in a radiating chapel on the
ambulatory behind the presbytery. The
baroque painter included a self-portrait in
the picture – the figure in the middle, beside
the soliform (sun-shaped) monstrance

In 1728, BRANDL WAS under house arrest in Hradec Králové for non-payment of his debts. He was released by the then abbot of Sedlec Monastery, who offered him work – painting a picture for the main altar of the newly restored cathedral. Brandl stayed almost two years in Sedlec and, in addition to the impressive altarpiece *The Assumption of the Virgin Mary*, he produced another three paintings: *The Patrons of the Czech Lands*, *The Vision of St Lutgardis* and *St Juliana of Liège*.

Following the dissolution of the monastery, *The Assumption of the Virgin Mary* altarpiece was sold to St Lawrence's Church in Vysoké Mýto in 1787. Brandl's three other paintings stand in the radiating chapels of the ambulatory in Sedlec Cathedral.

Intriguingly, *The Patrons of the Czech Lands* includes Brandl's self-portrait in the centre, among the saints. A sketch for the painting *The Vision of St Lutgardis* was itself the inspiration for the baroque sculptor Matthias Bernard Braun, who used it as the basis for a sculptural group that can now be seen on the thirteenth pedestal on Charles Bridge in Prague. Brandl depicted St Juliana kneeling before the immensely valuable Sedlec Monstrance.

However, collaborating with Brandl was not easy. This is confirmed by records in period chronicles in which the abbot complains that the commission is taking disproportionately longer than planned, and that the painter is incapable of keeping to agreed deadlines. This was because Brandl spent his time in Kutná Hora's taverns instead of working, cunningly stuffing his painter's trousers and hanging them from the scaffolding below half-finished paintings, to give the abbot the impression that he was hard at work.

Brandl returned to Kutná Hora in 1734 and died there on 24 September 1735. The place of his demise was symbolic – he died in a tavern during a wild drinking binge.

The painting *The Vision of St Lutgardis* (*c.*1729) by Petr Brandl, in a chapel on the ambulatory behind the presbytery

The painting *St Juliana of Liège* (*c.*1729) by Petr Brandl, in a chapel on the ambulatory behind the presbytery

12   THE CHAPEL OF OUR LADY OF SEDLEC

THE CHAPEL OF OUR LADY OF SEDLEC, in the cathedral's south aisle, has two altars and dates from the second half of the fifteenth century. The chapel's ground plan and the baroque paintings on its walls seem to transform it into another aisle in the cathedral, while its two altars highlight the particular reverence in which the Cistercians hold the Mother of God.

An interesting feature of this chapel is the once-gothic statue of the Virgin Mary, which was remodelled during the Baroque reconstruction by Judas Thaddaeus Supper. In addition to the chapel, he painted frescoes on the walls of Sedlec Monastery's refectory, covering an area of almost 2,000 square metres.

If you take a closer look at the Sedlec Madonna, as the statue is also called, you will notice that she has no hair – it was removed during the baroque-era modifications. In all probability, wigs were put on the statue on special occasions, although these have not been preserved.

The Chapel of Our Lady of Sedlec in the cathedral's south aisle has two altars; the statue of the Sedlec Madonna is located on the second altar

OPPOSITE: The original gothic statue of the Virgin Mary of Sedlec was remodelled in the 18th century into baroque form.

13   THE SEDLEC MONSTRANCE

THE ORIGINAL SEDLEC MONSTRANCE is on display in the treasury of the Cathedral of the Assumption of Our Lady. One of the oldest gothic monstrances in the world, it was probably made prior to 1389 by the Parler workshop, and was a commission from the archbishop of Prague, Jan of Jenštejn.

Another, almost certainly untrue, legend is associated with the immensely valuable monstrance: 'Late afternoon on a beautiful summer's day in 1702, the Kutná Hora master executioner went out to hunt birds. He noticed that an entire flock of jackdaws was sitting on the projections of the ruined cathedral façade. He fired at them, but missed, and instead of his prey, he hit the flaking plaster. This came loose and fell to the ground, and something gleamed gold beneath it in the light of the setting sun. It transpired that the precious monstrance had been hidden in a secret niche there. The chronicles even describe his reward for this successful hunting trip. The Kutná Hora executioner and his later successors were to receive a cart of hay and a cart of aftergrass (grass grown after the first crop of hay is harvested) from the monastery's meadows every year in perpetuity.'[5]

The tale is unlikely to be true because the monstrance, along with other valuable artefacts, appears in the inventory of liturgical objects that were removed when the Hussite Wars began, and hidden in a monastery in Klosterneuburg, Austria. In the nineteenth century, after the monastery was dissolved, the monstrance was transported from Sedlec to Vienna, where the intention was to melt it down to mint coins. Fortunately, however, it was spared because of its flawless design. The original monstrance was returned to Sedlec Cathedral in 2011.

The Sedlec Monstrance was made of silver and was then fire-gilded. It is 97 centimetres tall, weighs 4.7 kilograms and is one of the most important pieces of medieval goldsmithery in the Czech Republic.

The staircase which originally led from the cathedral loft directly into the monastery. One legend tells that Abbot James, carrying the monstrance, fled up here, away from Hussite troops. The staircase is currently impassable

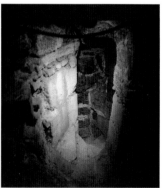

OPPOSITE: The original Sedlec Monstrance (a reliquary, pre-1389) is one of the oldest surviving gothic monstrances in the world. Monstrances are a special type of reliquary that display the transubstantiated host

14   SEDLEC MONASTERY DORMITORY

The original gothic dormitory and prelature building used to stand on the opposite side of the dormitory church, to the south, but was destroyed in 1421 by Hussite troops. The current dormitory was created when the monastery was reconstructed as a baroque building. However, the project was never fully completed as money ran out in 1765. At that time, forty-eight Cistercians lived in the dormitory's extensive grounds.

When the monastery was dissolved, the dormitory was used as a warehouse for flour, then as a warehouse for the Imperial woollen goods factory; later, it housed a military hospital. In 1812, a tobacco factory was established there, which initially manufactured snuff and pipe tobacco, then cigars and cigarettes. Over time, further necessary lean-to buildings were added to the original dormitory for product storage, although most of these were removed after 1992.

The remnants of a gothic portal are preserved in a passageway beside the cathedral. The portal may have

BELOW LEFT:
The exterior of
Sedlec Monastery
dormitory

The remnants of a
gothic portal, known as
the Gate of the Dead

been the one through which deceased monks were carried to the burial ground near the cathedral and is hence known as the Gate of the Dead.

Located behind the cathedral is the dormitory building with refectory, which is dominated by a tall tower. It was probably designed by Jan Blažej Santini Aichel.

LEFT: The ambulatory with radiating chapels in the Cathedral of the Assumption of Our Lady (view from the dormitory); part of the restored monastery garden in the foreground

ABOVE: View of the dormitory building from the ambulatory with radiating chapels; part of the restored monastery garden in the foreground

RIGHT: The corridor that originally connected the dormitory with the cathedral

BELOW: View of the ceiling in the former dormitory of Sedlec Monastery, which is one of the oldest reinforced concrete ceilings in the modern Czech Republic (early 20th century)

The refectory in the east wing has two floors, with an ambulatory on the first floor; the ground floor was intended for dining, while the monks had direct access to their cells from the gallery. The refectory is adorned with frescos by Judas Thaddaeus Supper, who with his assistants decorated an area of 2,000 square metres. The staircase, another designed by Jan Blažej Santini Aichel, is also remarkable. The south wing adjoins what is probably the oldest part of the monastery, known as the Abbot's Chapel.

As it houses the Philip Morris offices, the dormitory is not open to the public (see p. 28).

The Abbot's Chapel on the premises of the former Sedlec Monastery was used by the abbots for private prayer. The baroque stucco on the ceiling (early 18th century) was designed by Jan Blažej Santini Aichel

ABOVE: The entrance staircase from the refectory ambulatory, decorated with frescos (first half of the 18th century) by Judas Thaddaeus Supper

BELOW AND OVERLEAF: The two floors of the refectory with the first-floor ambulatory, decorated with frescos (first half of the 18th century) by Judas Thaddaeus Supper

15 ALL SAINTS CHURCH AND OSSUARY

THE CHURCH AND OSSUARY were built in the first half of the fourteenth century as a gothic two-storey charnel house, and from the outset the Sedlec Cistercians planned to use the space as a reverential repository for exhumed bones. This is also why the lower chapel is situated below ground level. The church was located in the northern part of the monastery grounds, in the centre of an extensive cemetery.

The roof and loadings of the entire church were probably damaged in 1421, during the Hussite Wars, but it was not restored until 1661–63, when it was already on the verge of complete collapse. This restoration saw the church's lower chapel enclosed by extensive buildings, more than tripling its area.

Another important historical milestone occurred at the turn of the seventeenth and eighteenth centuries, when the abbot, Jindřich Snopek, successfully obtained sufficient funds to restore the monastery. He invited Jan Blažej Santini Aichel to take on the project-architect role; Santini Aichel restored the cathedral, along with the already significantly dilapidated All Saints Church, in the spirit of baroque-gothic. The design of the first skeletal decorations in the ossuary's lower chapel is also ascribed to Santini Aichel.

View from the south-west of All Saints Church and Ossuary, surrounded by the cemetery, which is still in use

The upper chapel was originally covered by a gothic star vault and all the windows contained stained glass. The current vault dates from the baroque reconstruction

The church's upper chapel, located directly above the ossuary

In 1783, after the Cistercian monastery was dissolved, the Schwarzenberg family became the church's patrons. Over the nineteenth century, they financed the extensive reconstruction of the ossuary, including restoring and completing the skeletal decorations – the work of František Rint. The repairs were completed in 1870 and, for a long time, this was the last large investment in maintaining the monument. The church gradually fell into disrepair in the twentieth century. Restoration recommenced in 2014 and is planned to continue until around 2030.

View of All Saints Church and Ossuary from the Schwarzenberg mansion, over the original perimeter wall of the mansion grounds

16 SKELETAL REMAINS AND THE DECORATION OF SEDLEC OSSUARY

THE SKELETAL REMAINS NOW reposing in the ossuary's lower chapel come from cleared graves in Sedlec Cemetery. In the fourteenth century, Kutná Hora was an important mining town, which some sources claim had a population of up to 80,000 people. In 1318, Kutná Hora was struck by a famine, in which 20,000 of the city's inhabitants died, and thirty years later another approximately 30,000 inhabitants died of the plague. In the early fifteenth century, fighting in the Hussite Wars took place in the environs of Kutná Hora, and about a further 10,000 people lost their lives. All these people, and of course others from Kutná Hora who also died, were laid to rest in Sedlec Cemetery. However, when the cemetery had grown to an astonishing 3.5 hectares, the old fifteenth-century graves were exhumed and the bones were stored piecemeal round the perimeter wall of the lower chapel in All Saints Church. More graves were exhumed during subsequent outbreaks of plague, and finally – probably in the nineteenth century – Sedlec Cemetery was significantly reduced in size for the last time.

The suspended bone decorations in the lower chapel. The alternating skulls and thigh bones are meant to symbolise angels

Legend says that a half-blind monk was the first to stack the bones into six large pyramids, in 1511. Allegedly, his sight was miraculously restored when he finished this work. Today, however, we have no reliable documents recording when skeletal remains were first used to decorate the lower chapel. The architect Jan Blažej Santini Aichel is thought to have conceived and designed the current bone decorations in the spirit of baroque piety and in line with baroque aesthetic principles. The four pyramids of bones and skulls, the angel to the right of the crossing and all the ossuary's stucco decorations probably date from the Baroque period, but František Rint made very substantial changes to the baroque principles of Santini's decoration in the nineteenth century, in the spirit of Romanticism.

OPPOSITE: The central part of the lower chapel in All Saints Church, view of the cones and the chandelier of human bones by František Rint (pre-1870)

17   BONE PYRAMIDS

ONE OF THE OSSUARY's dominant features – four pyramids of bones and skulls – may date back to the Baroque era. It is possible that there were originally six pyramids, but two of them were taken apart in the nineteenth century and put to use in other decorations in the lower chapel. The four large bone pyramids are now situated in the corners of the chapel, surmounted by carved, gilded crowns. Santini Aichel's stucco crown-of-thorns decorations can be seen on the ceiling above the north-west and south-east pyramids; a stucco star adorns the ceiling above the other two pyramids.

The pyramidal arrangement is not a random choice. In the symbolism of elementary geometrical shapes, the pyramid refers to the vertical axis connecting heaven and earth, and thus brings earthly reality under the authority of heavenly rule. The positioning of the gilded carved baroque crowns on the pyramid apexes complements and enhances this idea. The pyramid symbolism is interpreted as the equality of all people before the throne of God, regardless of skin colour or social position.

The north-western pyramid was the first to be taken apart, in 2019, to correct the subsidence. When this process was underway, it was discovered that the bones within the pyramid were divided into several levels; they were not interconnected, only carefully pieced together, and the pyramid is not entirely assembled, as was originally assumed, of bones. Some levels contain historical building debris and small bone fragments. The wooden structures round the pyramids are not load bearing, but were meant to complement the shape and were primarily decorative in function. Dendrochronological surveys of the wooden structures have ascertained that the wood dates back to the Baroque reconstruction. Therefore it is assumed that Jan Blažej Santini Aichel either reassembled the pyramids or was the first to build them.

18   FRANTIŠEK RINT (1835–?)

In the history of Sedlec Ossuary, František Rint remains a somewhat mysterious figure. Although he was the craftsman who gave the lower chapel its modern form, how he came to Sedlec and who approached him to take up an occupation as unusual as bone decoration are questions that remain unanswered. František Rint, listed in the parish registers as a master saddler, came from České Skalice, in northern Bohemia, where he was celebrated for his artistic skill – he constructed a figure of the Imperial Austrian eagle from weapons and military supplies left behind after the Austro-Prussian War (1866). This remarkable work even attracted the interest and admiration of Emperor Franz Joseph I.

In any case, František Rint dismantled Santini Aichel's original strictly spiritual baroque concept and created decorations in the melancholy, mysterious spirit of Romanticism. While the baroque bone decorations used skulls and thigh bones exclusively, Rint incorporated other types of human bone into his adornments.

Rint created the most famous decorative elements – the chandelier, the Schwarzenberg coat-of-arms and the suspended garlands. The sole purely 'temporal' decoration is the Schwarzenberg family's coat-of-arms; in the lower right field you can see the motif of a rook (or raven) on the head of a Turkish warrior, recalling Adolf of Schwarzenberg's victory over the Ottoman troops at the fortress of Raab. The coat-of-arms is composed of bones of various sizes, which are attached to the wooden board with steel wires.

Rint's decorations gave the space a new, Romantic–macabre aspect and foregrounded the theme of death.

ABOVE: The signature of František Rint made in bones, including the completion date for the ossuary decorations (1870)

OPPOSITE: The Schwarzenberg coat-of-arms by František Rint (pre-1870) hanging on a wooden structure beside one of the pyramids in the lower chapel of All Saints Church

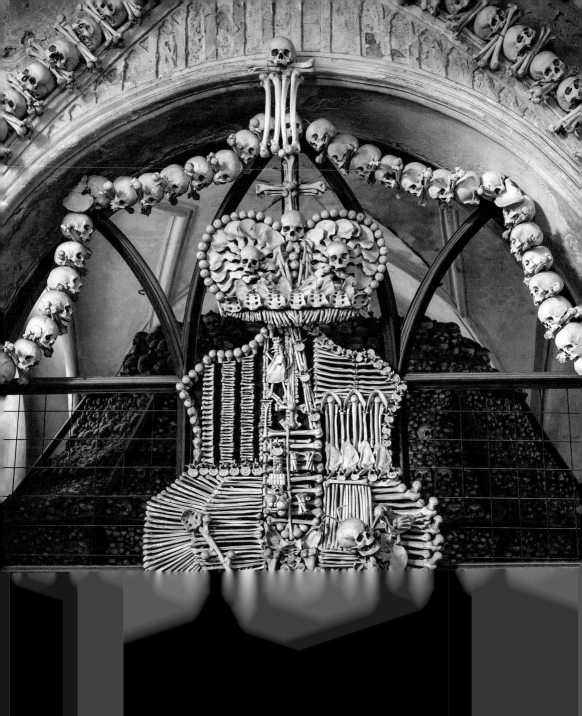

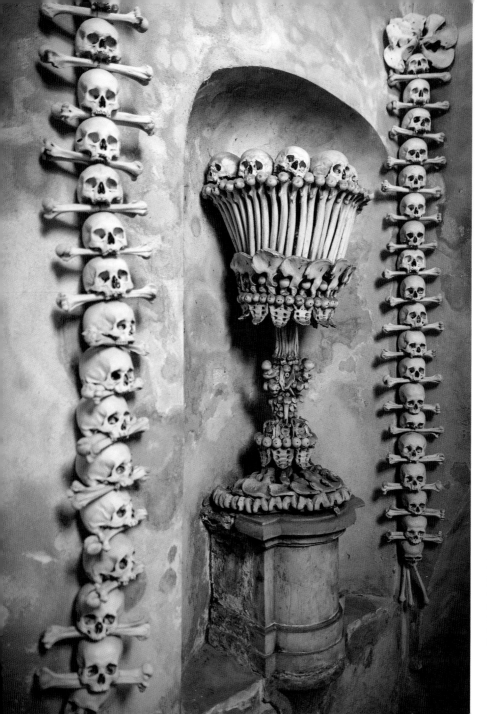

A chalice made of
bones from František
Rint's workshop (pre-
1870), situated in an
alcove on the left of
the central staircase
that leads into the
lower chapel

19   CHRISTIAN SYMBOLS AND MEMENTO MORI

THE PURPOSE OF BONE decorations in the lower chapel is to remind the living of the constant presence of death, but these also express the Christian hope of resurrection and the idea that death need not be the end. Sedlec Ossuary is based, then, on an important moral principle – memento mori – which was often cited in the Middle Ages and which warns human beings not to forget their transience and to prepare for death during their lives.

When visitors stand face-to-face with the dead in the ossuary, they should realise that one day they too will stand, with their deeds, before God. After death, they will no longer be able to mend their ways and do good works. This consideration should lead them to change their lives while they still have time. At the same time, the Bible states that the dead

BELOW LEFT: Decorations in the church vestibule with the letters IHS – *Iesus Hominum Salvator* (Jesus the Saviour of Humankind).

BELOW RIGHT: A cone in the central part of the lower chapel, decorated with human skulls and carved wooden angels

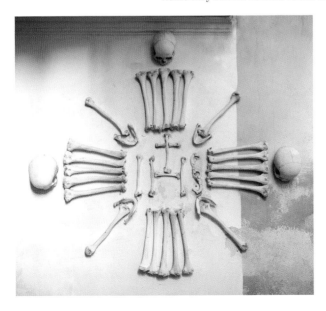

The presbytery with altar in the lower chapel of All Saints Church. Bone monstrances from František Rint's workshop are situated along the side walls (pre-1870); the baroque stucco on the ceiling is by Jan Blažej Santini Aichel (early 18th century)

OPPOSITE: A bone monstrance by František Rint (1870)

will be raised, both body and soul, at the Last Judgement, to eternal life. Thus, they see the deceased waiting for this moment, and so this assembly of the dead visibly reflects the hope with which they will be buried: that Christ's death and resurrection means that they will one day rise with him.

Other Christian symbols made of bone serve to emphasise God's message. We can see the Greek letters iota, eta and sigma on both side walls by the entrance to the vestibule. These are the first letters of the word *IÉSÚS*, the Greek form of Jesus. On the opposite walls are the initials *IHS*, which is the Latin abbreviation of *Iesus Hominum Salvator* – Jesus the Saviour of Humankind (or of sinners). The cross on the front wall of the vestibule and the chalices in the alcoves by the staircase are also Christian symbols. The chalice and monstrance are a reference to the Eucharist, the bread of life; the cross is a sign of victory over death, symbolising God's power and wisdom.

THE RESTORATION OF SEDLEC OSSUARY

ALL SAINTS CHURCH AND OSSUARY has been undergoing extensive repairs since 2014. The ossuary was declared structurally unsound after 1989. No substantial investment had been made into maintaining it during the twentieth century. The biggest long-term problem is subsidence, which probably began in the period of the Hussite Wars and which is causing the western part of the church to lean by almost 50 centimetres from perpendicular. A second major problem was the high levels of damp in the lower chapel, as a result of which the bone decorations, plaster and stucco

TOP LEFT AND BELOW:
The current condition
of plaster in the lower
chapel

ABOVE: The current condition of stucco decorations and plaster in the lower chapel

LEFT: The current condition of plaster in the lower chapel; the hanging bone decorations have, however, already been restored

had gradually fallen down, the altar had crumbled and the walls had cracked.

Unusually, the monument's administrator, the Roman Catholic parish of Kutná Hora – Sedlec, decided to finance the ossuary reconstruction purely from tourist income, rather than from subsidies, grants or funds. The reason was the highly demanding nature of the restoration and the need to decide freely on deadlines and suppliers without excessive administrative burdens. That this decision was the correct one is evident by the restoration of the bone decorations, because bone is an exceptional material that must be approached with piety and humility.

More than 90 million Czech crowns (almost 4 million euros) had been invested by the end of 2022. The roof, rafters and terraces have all been repaired; the church's subsidence has been partly corrected; and the bone decorations are undergoing repairs – including the first of the four pyramids, which has been taken apart and reassembled. There has been an extensive archaeological survey of the area round the ossuary, which has uncovered more than 1,800 complete burials including mass graves dating back to previous plagues and famines (see pp. 7, 60).

The reconstruction of the ossuary is due to be completed in or around 2030. The ossuary has been open to the public for the entire restoration period to ensure there are sufficient funds to allow the work to continue.

ABOVE: The exterior of All Saints Church and Ossuary is now almost fully restored

LEFT: The main altar in the lower chapel in its current state

OVERLEAF: One of the bone pyramids in its current state

21　THE PARISH OF SEDLEC TODAY

THE HISTORY OF THE former Cistercian monastery in Sedlec is convoluted, dramatic and, at times, tragic. The fate of the vast majority of the tens of thousands of people associated with this place has long been forgotten. Today, a visitor who finds the time to slow down, contemplate and listen attentively may be able to recall a few names. This visitor must also be open to the silent question that constantly vibrates through this sacred space: 'All this has been left here by us, the bearers of hope in a life that death cannot end. What is your hope, pilgrim? What will you leave for future generations?'

We bear the heritage of our ancestors, and are driven by the responsibility and the desire to hand it down to our successors in the best condition possible. Like many before us, and maybe many after us, we come to this holy place to praise God, pray and ask for His blessing on all people and every individual separately. Aware of our mission, we are creating a living Christian society, with Jesus Christ, crucified and resurrected, at its heart. We regularly celebrate Mass for those who, many generations ago, lived and worked here, prayed, suffered, experienced happy moments, and died; for those who found their final resting place here; for those who come today in faith, or maybe with curiosity; and for all our benefactors. We also pray to God without ceasing for those who come to pray in the cathedral.

We use the premises of Sedlec Cathedral and Ossuary for a great many cultural and artistic events, from exhibitions to concerts and theatrical performances to educational and adventure programmes.

Father Pavel Tobek, priest of Sedlec parish

View of the main altar of Sedlec Cathedral at the spring equinox. The builders of the original gothic cathedral so constructed it that the rays of the setting sun shine through the largest window on the west façade directly onto the symbolic heart of the sacred building – the main altar – at the spring and autumn equinoxes

This edition © Scala Arts & Heritage Publishers Ltd, 2023
Text © Radka Krejčí, Pavel Tobek, 2023. Photography © Ondřej Soukup, 2023

Scala Arts & Heritage Publishers Ltd
305 Access House, 141–157 Acre Lane London,
SW2 5UA, United Kingdom
www.scalapublishers.com

In partnership with the Roman Catholic parish of Kutná Hora – Sedlec Zámecká
127, 284 03 Kutná Hora, Czech Republic
www.sedlec.info

Editor and project manager: Kateřina Siegl
Designed by Matthew Wilson
Translation: Isabel Stainsby. Editing: Robert Anderson
in association with First Edition Translations Ltd, Cambridge, UK
Printed and bound in the Czech Republic

ISBN: 978-17-8551-475-3
First edition 2023
10 9 8 7 6 5 4 3 2 1

Endnotes

1 J. Jelínková, *Staré/nové kutnohorské pověsti* [Old and New Legends of Kutná Hora]
   (Kutná Hora, 2017), p. 53.

2 Ibid., p. 55.

3 Ibid., p. 7.

4 Ibid., p. 59.

5 Ibid., p. 60.

With thanks to Philip
Morris ČR a.s., the
Roman Catholic
parish and deanery
of Vysoké Mýto, Karel
Schwarzenberg and
Karel Vopařil for their
help and support for
this book.

FRONT COVER: The
Schwarzenberg coat-of-
arms by František Rint
(pre-1870) hanging on a
wooden structure beside
one of the pyramids in the
lower chapel of All Saints
Church

BACK COVER: The
presbytery with altar
in the upper chapel of
All Saints Church and
Ossuary; a restored
baroque positive
(portable) organ stands
on the left

FRONT FLAP: The
dextrorotatory staircase
leading to the transept,
one of the most important
architectural elements
contributed by Jan Blažej
Santini Aichel (early 18th
century)

pp. 2–3: Sedlec Cathedral's
ambulatory with radiating
chapels, viewed from the
former dormitory; the
cloister garden is in the
foreground, the former
monastery buildings are
to the sides